Start with Art

Collages

Isabel Thomas

Heinemann Library
Chicago, Illinois

www.heinemannraintree.com
Visit our website to find out more information about Heinemann-Raintree books.

To order:
☎ Phone 888-454-2279
💻 Visit www.heinemannraintree.com to browse our catalog and order online.

© 2012 Heinemann Library
an imprint of Capstone Global Library, LLC
Chicago, Illinois

Edited by Dan Nunn, Rebecca Rissman, and Catherine Veitch
Designed by Richard Parker
Picture research by Mica Brancic and Hannah Taylor
Originated by Capstone Global Library
Printed and bound in the United States of America,
  North Mankato, MN

15 14 13 12
10 9 8 7 6 5 4 3 2

Library of Congress Cataloging-in-Publication Data
Thomas, Isabel, 1980-
  Collages / Isabel Thomas.—1st ed.
     p. cm.—(Start with art)
  Includes bibliographical references and index.
  ISBN 978-1-4329-5020-0 (hardcover)—ISBN 978-1-4329-5027-9 (pbk.) 1. Collage—Technique—Juvenile literature. I. Title.
  N7433.7.T48 2011
  702.81'2—dc22   2010042681

012012
006539RP

Acknowledgments
We would like to thank the following for permission to reproduce photographs: © Capstone Publishers pp. 5, 8, 10, 20, 21, 22, 23 – materials (Karon Dubke); Corbis pp. 9 (Albright-Knox Art Gallery), 12 (© Images.com/Gerald Bustamante), 19 (The Art Archive); Getty Images p. 6 (Matt Cardy); Jo Brooker pp. 7, 23 – fabric; Shutterstock pp. 11 (© Studio DMM Photography, Designs & Art), 23 – gallery (© Shamleen), 23 – mosaic (© tratong), 23 – self-portrait (© re_bekka), 23 – texture (© Konstantin Sutyagin); Tate Images pp. 15, 18 (© Tate); The Bridgeman Art Library pp. 4 (© Sarah Hammond. All rights reserved, DACS 2011), 13 (Private Collection/© ADAGP, Paris and DACS, London 2011/Giraudon), 14 (Private Collection), 16 (The Israel Museum, Jerusalem, Israel/© Romare Bearden Foundation/DACS, London/VAGA, New York 2011/Gift of Mr and Mrs Gerhard, New York), 17 (Roy Miles Fine Paintings/Private Collection).

Front cover photograph of Trafalgar Square (collage) by William Cooper reproduced with permission of The Bridgeman Art Library (Private Collection). Back cover photograph of a child looking through a magazine reproduced with permission of © Capstone Publishers (Karon Dubke). Back cover photograph of a child using glue reproduced with permission of © Capstone Publishers (Karon Dubke).

Every effort has been made to contact copyright holders of material reproduced in this book. Any omissions will be rectified in subsequent printings if notice is given to the publisher.

Contents

Some words are shown in bold, **like this**. You can find out what they mean by looking in the glossary.

What Is a Collage?

Many artists make collages.

A collage is a picture made by sticking different things on to paper, canvas, or cardboard.

You can be an artist, too.

A girl has made this collage by sticking paper onto cardboard.

Where Can I See Collages?

Some collages are displayed in museums and **galleries**.

Everyone can go and look at them.

You can see collages in books and magazines, too.

This collage shows you what the people in a story look like.

What Do People Use to Make Collages?

You can use almost anything to make a collage.

Cut or tear up paper, collect **fabric** scraps, and look for **materials** outside.

Try making art with things that would usually be thrown away.

This collage was made with old wallpaper, newspapers, and magazines.

How Do People Make Collages?

Artists start by planning their collage.

They arrange different **materials** to make a picture.

When they are happy with the picture, they glue everything down.

This artist overlapped materials to give her picture **texture**.

How Do People Use Shapes in Collages?

This collage shows a picture of a flower.

The artist used rectangle shapes for the flower's petals.

Different objects have been glued onto paper to make this picture.

How many different shapes can you see in this picture?

What Can Collages Show?

A collage can show real things.

Artists make collages of people, buildings, and objects.

Art can show ideas, too. This collage is about movement.

Can you spot a soccer player's legs, a spacecraft, and an airplane?

How Can Collages Show Feelings?

Artists use shapes and colors to show feelings.

Gray, green, and blue colors in this picture make people feel calm.

Bright colors make us feel happy.

Which colors make you feel happy in this collage?

What Other Types of Collage Are There?

Art can be very small or very big.

This collage is made from big pieces of wood that washed up on a beach.

A **mosaic** is like a collage made of small pieces of stone.

The Romans used mosaics to decorate floors.

Start to Make Collages!

Many artists use newspaper and magazine clippings in their collages. Try making a funny **self-portrait** using **materials** you find.

1. Collect old magazines, newspapers, wrapping paper, and pieces of **fabric**.

2. Find a large picture to be the background for your self-portrait.

3. Cut a face shape and hand shapes out of colored paper.

4. Cut a mouth, eyes, hair, and clothes from the materials that you collected. Arrange them to make a new picture – of yourself!

5. Add objects to show your favorite hobbies and toys.

6. When you are happy with your collage, glue everything down.

Glossary

fabric soft, bendy material, such as cloth. Clothes are made from fabric.

gallery place where art is displayed for people to look at

materials things you can use to make art

mosaic design made by pasting many small colored objects together

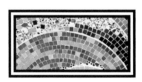

self-portrait picture that you draw or make of yourself

texture how something feels when you touch it

Find Out More

Book

Thomas, Isabel. *Making Collage (Action Art)*.
Chicago: Heinemann-Raintree, 2005.

Websites

Take a fun tour of modern art on this Website:
www.moma.org/interactives/destination/

Visit this Website to find more ideas for making collages:
kids.tate.org.uk/create/make_a_collage.shtm

Index